TEN PRINCIPLES
for a Successful Marriage

TEN PRINCIPLES
for a Successful Marriage

Practical Lessons from the Ten Commandments

Mac and Amy McNair

CUMBERLAND HOUSE
NASHVILLE, TENNESSEE

Published by Cumberland House Publishing, Inc.
431 Harding Industrial Drive, Nashville, TN 37211.

Cover design by Unlikely Suburban Design; Text design by Lisa Taylor

Scripture quotations are from the HOLY BIBLE, NEW INTERNATIONAL VERSION. Copyright © 1973, 1978, 1984 by International Bible Society. Used by permission of Zondervan Bible Publishing House. All rights reserved.

Library of Congress Cataloging-in-Publication Data

McNair, Mac, 1923–
    Ten principles for a successful marriage : practical lessons from the Ten commandments / Mac and Amy McNair.

       p.   cm.
    ISBN 1-58182-022-4 (pbk. : alk. paper)
    1. Spouses—Religious life.   2. Marriage—Religious aspects—Christianity.
3. Ten commandments—Criticism, interpretation, etc.   I. McNair, Amy,
1922– .   II. Title.   III. Title: 10 principles for a successful marriage.
BV4596.M3M45   1999
248.8'44—dc21   99-12213
                                                          CIP

Printed in the United States of America
1 2 3 4 5 6 7 8 — 03 02 01 00 99

To our parents, our two children,
and our nine grandchildren. We love them
dearly and pray for them regularly.

CONTENTS

PREFACE

Several years ago my secretary asked me to speak at her wedding ceremony. She was almost like a daughter to me, so I agreed to do so. When I told Amy about it, she asked me what I was going to say. I didn't know.

"Why don't you talk about the ten principles for a successful marriage?" she said.

"What are they?" I responded.

Of course, I knew what she meant—the application of the biblical Ten Commandments to marriage. I had just finished a training program for business people on the application of the ten principles for business based on the Ten Commandments, but hadn't considered their application to marriage. So I began to develop what you will discover in this little book.

Amy and I have succeeded in more than fifty years of marriage by relying on principles that at first seemed like just common courtesy—common sense. On closer inspection, however, we saw that these principles are inspired by the Ten Commandments.

Then, as we studied the Commandments more closely, we were inspired to apply them to other areas of our lives.

We were truly amazed, so many years ago, by all the possible applications of God's Word when we allowed them to be written on our hearts, not just in stone.

PHOTOGRAPH ACKNOWLEDGMENTS

Thanks to all the couples whose photos appear in the book. May their long-lived marriages be an inspiration to readers. And special thanks to Shirley Seput for her help in collecting photos.

TEN PRINCIPLES
for a Successful Marriage

INTRODUCTION

MAC: When the new neighbors moved in next door, I paid little attention to them because I was finishing high school and working to save money to go to the University of Alabama. I wanted to get my degree in aeronautical engineering; my dream was to fly airplanes.

I had dreamed of flying airplanes since I was six years old. Charles Lindbergh was my hero. If you had known me then—a barefoot boy in overalls with a severe speech impediment—you would have thought it an impossible dream. Nevertheless, I had the dream, and I kept it to myself.

Shortly after the next door neighbors moved in, my mother sent me over to take them something to welcome them to the neighborhood. I discovered there were seven kids in the family, and one of them was a cute girl, just a year behind me in high school. I paid her little attention, and she paid me little attention. But when she started attending the church where I went, and then my high school, we began to notice each other.

I didn't start off too well with her.

AMY: "Didn't start off too well" is an understatement. I

thought Mac was arrogant, aggressive, pushy, and too sure of himself. One day I was embroidering a pillowcase for my hope chest when he came over. He took one look at it and asked me what it was. When I told him, he said, "Someday I'll lay my head on that pillowcase."

"Never!" I responded. Well, I stuck to my word, because I've kept that pillowcase in my hope chest ever since.

But as we began to date, I discovered some attributes about Mac that I liked very much. When I was sixteen, he asked me to marry him, and I cried. He asked me why I was crying, and I said, "Because I don't want to leave my mother."

5

"You don't have to do that," he said. "I have to finish high school and go to college and get a job."

Then I cried again because I didn't want to wait that long. And when World War II came along after he graduated high school, I didn't know how long we would have to wait.

MAC: The War created an opportunity for me to fulfill my childhood dream. I had been accepted to the University, but instead I joined the Army Air Corps and went through the aviation cadet program at Maxwell Air Force Base.

Then I began my flying training at the Embry-Riddle School of Aviation at Arcadia, Florida.

For a year I was so busy Amy and I saw very little of each other. But we were together just long enough for me to give her an engagement ring during my final month of flight training. Shortly after I received my wings and my "bars" as a second lieutenant, I was stationed at Meridian, Mississippi. I called Amy and said, "Let's get married."

"But the War is on," she said.

"That's right," I said, "but let's get married. Pack your bags and come to Meridian."

She did. She arrived at the train depot wearing a cute little hat and all dressed up, carrying that hope chest. I had planned a chapel wedding, but it didn't work out. Then I had planned a wedding with a local Baptist pastor, but that didn't work out either.

It appeared we would have to spend the night together, and since our values wouldn't allow us to do that unless we were married, we found a judge to marry us that night. He was in his pajamas and the taxi driver was our witness, on April 27, 1943.

Our life quickly became a whirlwind of activities as I

was transferred to Greenville, South Carolina, then to Europe where by November 1943 I was with the 363rd fighter group as a 19-year-old P-51 pilot. I was gone for a little more than two years, and was shot down twice during that time. A lot of letters crossed the Atlantic between Amy and me. I experienced a lot of lonely moments and did a lot of praying, and I know Amy did the same.

AMY: In addition to writing and praying, I went with my sister-in-law and her husband and their small child, at my father's request, to the Bremington, Washington, shipyards, where I worked for a while. Then I came back South and worked at the Ordnance Plant in Bossier City, Louisiana. Mac's activity in the war caused my faith in God to grow stronger and stronger.

MAC: Many may wonder how we kept things together during this long absence from one another. Well, Amy and I have opposite personalities. She has the gift of mercy and compassion, and I don't. I'm high control and I want to run the show. She doesn't like criticism, but when things don't go my way, I criticize. You see the potential for conflict?

But we had a common set of values—values based on principles that are more than 3,000 years old. They were taught to us by our parents.

What principles? The principles that Moses brought down off the mountain top. The Ten Commandments.

1. I AM THE LORD YOUR GOD, WHO BROUGHT YOU OUT OF EGYPT, OUT OF THE LAND OF SLAVERY. YOU SHALL HAVE NO OTHER GODS BEFORE ME.

2. YOU SHALL NOT MAKE FOR YOURSELF AN IDOL IN THE FORM OF ANYTHING IN HEAVEN OR ABOVE OR ON EARTH BENEATH OR IN THE WATERS BELOW.

3. YOU SHALL NOT MISUSE THE NAME OF THE LORD YOUR GOD, FOR THE LORD WILL NOT HOLD ANYONE GUILTLESS WHO MISUSES HIS NAME.

4. REMEMBER THE SABBATH DAY BY KEEPING IT HOLY. SIX DAYS YOU SHALL LABOR AND DO ALL YOUR WORK, BUT THE SEVENTH DAY IS A SABBATH TO THE LORD YOUR GOD.

5. HONOR YOUR FATHER AND MOTHER, SO THAT YOU MAY LIVE LONG IN THE LAND THE LORD YOUR GOD IS GIVING YOU.

6. YOU SHALL NOT MURDER.

7. YOU SHALL NOT COMMIT ADULTERY.

8. YOU SHALL NOT STEAL.

9. YOU SHALL NOT GIVE FALSE TESTIMONY AGAINST YOUR NEIGHBOR.

10. YOU SHALL NOT COVET YOUR NEIGHBOR'S HOUSE. YOU SHALL NOT COVET YOUR NEIGHBOR'S WIFE, OR HIS MANSERVANT OR MAIDSERVANT, HIS OX OR DONKEY, OR ANYTHING THAT BELONGS TO YOUR NEIGHBOR.

During those early years of marriage, the world probably would not have considered us very good Christians. We didn't go to church much. Nevertheless, those principles kept us together. We assumed our responsibility to each other and behaved responsibly. And regardless of the conflicts that arose as a result of personality differences, our love began to grow and grow. Now, more than 50 years later, we love each other more than we ever did.

How did we apply the principles of the Ten Commandments to our marriage? That's what this book is all about. And when you study the Ten Commandments further, you will realize the principles can touch every aspect of your life.

One more personal note: We wanted children in our family, but were unable to have them. So after eleven years together we decided to adopt a lovely little girl, and a few years later we adopted a lovely little boy. Today those two children have given us nine wonderful grandchildren. Needless to say, we know that our children and our grandchildren are truly a gift from God.

The 1st Commandment...

I AM THE LORD YOUR GOD, WHO BROUGHT YOU OUT OF EGYPT, OUT OF SLAVERY. YOU SHALL HAVE NO OTHER GODS BEFORE ME.

— 1 —
Respect Each Other's Position of Authority

Authority, like responsibility, seems to be a despised word these days. Nobody wants to take responsibility. Nobody wants to give authority. But a marriage cannot succeed without respect for authority.

Many people who dislike the word *authority* believe it calls for one person to always be under the rule of another. They think of authority as being unilateral. But authority is three dimensional. It goes up, down, and collateral. Let me explain.

The military has, perhaps, the most widely recognized, and often misunderstood, lines of authority. For those who do understand it, however, military authority can offer a valuable corollary for the family.

Take the Air Force as an example. A successful general understands and respects the authority of the sergeant. Therefore, even though his rank allows it, he avoids giving direct orders to an airman. That's the sergeant's job.

Likewise, in the marriage a husband and wife divide the areas over which each will hold authority. Once that division of authority is recognized, each spouse should respect it.

That said, we should also understand that times arise

when one person must assume ultimate authority within the family. When we come to an impasse, somebody has to make a decision. Continuing with the military analogy, the general decides whether to attack or retreat. But he doesn't make that decision until he has complete input from the officers under his command. Amy recognizes that this ultimate authority lies with me, and I do not decide without her input.

Do not confuse the word *ultimate* with "complete," or "total" authority. I do not, and could not, make every decision in our family. And even though I do not necessarily agree with every decision that Amy makes, she's in charge of certain aspects of our family and is most capable in those areas.

In fact, at several stages of my Air Force career when the children were young, I was gone quite a bit on temporary duty over North Africa. And while I was gone, Amy knew that she had total authority over all our family matters. It made it easy on her because some husbands would never give their wives the authority, or even the checkbook for that matter.

Within our marriage, the ultimate—and this time I do mean complete and total—authority rests with God. He

John and Barbara the year they wed – December 1962 . . .

"A husband and wife [should] divide the areas over which each will hold authority. . . . Respecting each other's authority is one of the keys to a successful marriage."

. . . John and Barbara 36 years later.

leads us individually and as a family. But like the good general, even God respects our authority to make our own decisions. He respects our authority so much, in fact, that He will let us go to hell if we choose to.

Authority in our family does not end with Amy and me. Our children, when they were in our house, had authority over certain matters. For example, our daughter had a note on her door that said, Knock Before Entering, and I always did. Amy and I also considered their opinions when making decisions. Children should respect each other's authority as well. This minimizes sibling rivalry.

Authority is not the same thing as a dictatorship. Respecting each other's authority is one of the keys to a successful marriage.

The 2nd Commandment...

YOU SHALL NOT MAKE FOR YOURSELF
AN IDOL IN THE FORM OF ANYTHING IN
HEAVEN ABOVE OR ON EARTH BENEATH
OR IN THE WATERS BELOW.

— 2 —
Have Singleness
of Purpose
in Your Marriage

Put your spouse first among your earthly priorities. It's that simple. Career, children, and everything else must take a secondary role to your spouse's needs and interests. If the marriage is strong, the other areas will be strong as well.

God commanded, "You shall not make for yourself an idol in the form of anything in heaven above or on earth beneath or in the waters below."

How many times have you seen a mother who worships her children? She focuses all of her attention on them and says she is just fulfilling her role as a mother. At the same time, the father idolizes his career, committing all of

28

his time and energy to his work and fulfilling, as he sees it, his role as provider.

Each spouse is happy with their separate and rarely intersecting responsibilities. But eventually the children leave home and the man retires. Then the husband and wife look at one another across the table and realize they don't even know each other.

The key to marriage is companionship. If you make companionship the primary purpose of your marriage, you will grow continually closer.

For the first eleven years of our marriage, Amy and I

29

Robert and Virginia waiting at the dentist's office,
December, 1968, married 2 years . . .

"The key to marriage is companionship. If you make companionship the primary purpose of your marriage, you will grow continually closer."

. . . *Ginny and Bob 28 years later.*

had no children. We did everything together. I didn't go off with the boys to play golf. I played golf with Amy. In fact, I didn't join any men-only lodges, and she didn't join a garden club or Junior League. Instead, we took every opportunity to be together.

Of course, we had our times apart. Long times apart when Air Force duty took me to the other side of the world. But we created opportunities to be together. When I was in Vietnam for a year, for example, we met twice in Hawaii.

Later, when I started my management training career, many times clients needed me in cities where I could have flown. Because I wanted Amy with me and we couldn't afford two plane tickets, I drove and we spent that time together. Those long road trips provided us with wonderful opportunities to talk, to be together, to be companions. And even though we don't always like the same things— Amy loves baseball, but I don't—we do things together for companionship. When we lived in Chicago, we jogged together . . . again, companionship. The first priority of marriage.

Sex, the close physical relationship and the second priority of marriage, helps cement the marriage. Enjoy it. Just

33

Ernestine and Fred in 1945 on a belated honeymoon . . .

"Put your spouse first among your earthly priorities. Career, children, and everything else must take a secondary role to your spouse's needs and interests."

. . . 48 years later at Ernestine's 70th birthday party.

remember the sexual relationship starts in the morning in order to be fulfilled at night.

Bringing children into the world is, with God's blessing, the third objective in marriage. Without reproduction there is no future generation. Children should be discussed and agreed upon before the marriage. God's purpose is fulfilled through your children and your children's children.

The 3rd Commandment...

YOU SHALL NOT MISUSE THE NAME OF THE
LORD, FOR THE LORD WILL NOT HOLD
ANYONE GUILTLESS WHO MISUSES HIS NAME.

— 3 —
Practice Effective Communication

Americans have not been taught how to listen to others. We listen to ourselves talking, but we don't hear what others have to say.

A lady said to me, "My husband never talks to me."

I asked her, "Doesn't he ever take you out to dinner?"

"Yes, he does, but he's not there."

How frustrating and disheartening to be with someone who's "not there," especially when that person is your husband or wife.

We must communicate effectively. And we must know what our spouse needs to hear from us.

Practice Effective Communication

My wife wants me to tell her, "I love you." She knows I love her and I know I love her. Yet, she needs to hear me say it. So I do.

Marriage can be broken into three phases. Each phase requires different types of communication. During the honeymoon phase, when we're caught up in the romantic and emotional aspects of marriage, communication is not so important. We have not yet begun to notice the little things that will frustrate us later. The only time we communicate less is when we're dating. During these early years we're laying land mines—booby traps that have the potential to explode and seriously damage, or even wreck the marriage years down the road.

A couple came to me some years ago for advice in their marriage. We met for lunch and I could see quickly some obvious differences in them. She was a lovely young lady, dressed immaculately. He looked unkempt from his shoulders down to his sockless feet. We sat together over lunch and I started by asking the man his objective in getting married.

"So I could have somebody to sleep with," he said. "For sex."

His wife gasped. When she recovered I asked her the same question.

"To have someone who would love and care for me," she replied.

What two more opposite objectives could two people have in a marriage? He hadn't learned the meaning of "love and cherish."

Although most marriages do not bring together two such disparate points of view, over the course of the decades too many couples find themselves at least as far apart as this young couple. They sow more seeds during the second phase

Hardy and Jean in 1946 at St. Paul Bible College where they met . . .

> "God is preeminent above all things. . . . A husband and wife should, together, put God before all else."

. . . Hardy and Jean in 1982. They were married 35 years at the time of Hardy's death.

of marriage. They sacrifice so she can stay home with the children, but that means he focuses more on his career, works longer hours, and spends little quality time with his wife.

I spoke about marriage at a church one Sunday morning, and at the end of the service I said, "If your marriage needs working on from a communication standpoint, why don't you come down and kneel at the altar." Well, you would have thought it was a Billy Graham crusade. The pews were practically empty and people were lined up three and four deep at the altar. A moment later the minister came down from the pulpit and met his wife at the altar.

Since then I've come to realize that it is not uncommon for pastors to devote more time and attention to their ministries than to their wives. They think they're putting God as their first priority. But putting one's ministry ahead of the family isn't the same as making God the top priority. God is preeminent above all things—not a "priority." A husband and wife should, together, put God before all else. In their earthly business, however, the marriage and the family must always come before business, even if the business is a full-time ministry. To do otherwise is not biblical.

Mary and Patrick the year they were married – 1964 . . .

"Effective communication must begin early— before the marriage takes place. Talk to each other. Listen to each other. Tell each other when things are troubling you."

. . . *Mary and Patrick 34 years later.*

If you don't commit yourselves to communication during the early and middle stages of your marriage, you will find yourselves at retirement time, the children grown and gone, living with a stranger and wondering how such a thing could happen.

Effective communication must begin early—before the marriage takes place. Talk to each other. Listen to each other. Tell each other when things are troubling you. Do not run from conflict, but address it openly and honestly. Realize that resolving conflict is the price you pay for deeper intimacy. If your ultimate goal is to keep the marriage strong, then you will be motivated to keep lines of communication open.

The toughest time to talk can be at the end of the day. If the wife stays home, she's around children all day. When her husband comes in, she wants to talk. But when he comes home from work, he wants quiet. The key here is for the husband to understand that he isn't coming home from work. He's coming home to work, for his marriage and his family are infinitely more important than anything he will do all day.

One of the best books that I have ever read on this

principle was written by a Swiss psychiatrist, Dr. Paul Tourneir. It is called, *To Understand Each Other.* I highly recommend it. When you put this principle into practice, you will reach the point that just being in the same room together will be a form of communication.

The 4th Commandment...

REMEMBER THE SABBATH DAY BY
KEEPING IT HOLY. SIX DAYS YOU SHALL
LABOR AND DO ALL YOUR WORK, BUT
THE SEVENTH DAY IS A SABBATH TO
THE LORD YOUR GOD.

— 4 —

Maintain a Proper Balance Between Work and Rest

$\mathcal{I}$'ve never had a hobby. I don't take time to play golf when I could be reading a book. I don't fish. Work is my hobby. I call it play. And when I play at my work, I enjoy it. So I find practicing this principle most difficult.

God made it clear to us that He wants us to work six days and take a day off. We may think we'll be more successful if we work seven days, but Truett Cathy, founder of Chick-fil-A, has proved otherwise. His restaurants close on Sunday, and yet their success continues to grow.

The idea is simple. God designed a day off so he can re-create us. Worship. Reflect. Renew your marriage.

In our family, Amy needs a day off as much as I do. A couple should design their schedule so the wife can relax on Sunday as well. When I was growing up my mother prepared Sunday dinner on Saturday so she could relax on Sunday.

You're familiar with the tragic story of the workaholic businessman who provides a beautiful house for his family, a house at the lake, a boat, and fancy new cars. The wife busies herself with taking care of the home and the children, and the children grow up practically fatherless because their father is always working.

Each of you has a different role to play regarding work,

57

Caroline and Kevin in 1977 . . .

" . . . Get away together, just the two of you, once a year. Get to know each other again as adult individuals. Update your plan for your marriage. Regain your focus.

. . . married 24 years.

and you must help each other fulfill those responsibilities. Work together. But don't forget to take time to rest. That is important for your health and well-being as well as the well-being of your marriage.

In addition to resting one day a week, you should get away together, just the two of you, once a year. Get to know each other again as adult individuals. Update your plan for your marriage. Regain your focus.

Years ago, when Amy and I were living in Miami and I was gone to North Africa for three-month periods, I would come home and we would go up to Key Biscayne Beach, no more than fifteen minutes from our home. We would take the children and rent a villa for several days. It was an important time for us to come together again as a family and as a couple.

Over the years, whenever a major decision was pending, we would get away. Remember, we hear God not in the strong wind, not in the earthquake, not in the fire. Rather, he comes to us in the still small voice. To hear Him we must stop, be quiet, and listen.

The 5th Commandment...

HONOR YOUR FATHER AND MOTHER, SO
THAT YOU MAY LIVE LONG IN THE LAND
THE LORD YOUR GOD IS GIVING YOU.

— 5 —

*Show Respect for Elders
and Seek Counsel
from Those Who Are
Older and Wiser*

I believe every young couple should be required to live with a couple who have been married for fifty years or longer to see how much they depend on each other. We learn more by example than by instruction—even more, of course, by experience. But experience sometimes hurts, and we can avoid the pain if we seek and respect the counsel of our elders.

Amy and I have always had mentors. We were fortunate in that our parents lived until we were well into adulthood. They were there for us to turn to when we needed advice. Amy's mother lived to be 103, and my mother lived

Show Respect for Elders and Seek Counsel from Those Who Are Older and Wiser

to be 90. Not only did we call upon their wisdom, but we did everything we could to honor them.

Apparently, our parents taught us well, because our children and grandchildren often turn to us for advice and counsel. In addition to our family, young neighbors and friends come to Amy or me with difficult questions. Amy receives Mother's Day cards from young mothers around the country who have depended upon her advice. Neither of us claims any unique knowledge. We just offer the wisdom that only parents with a half-century of marriage can instill.

65

Show Respect for Elders and Seek Counsel from
Those Who Are Older and Wiser

Celcelia and Charles leaving the chapel,
february 27, 1949 . . .

> "Seek the counsel
> of your elders, and
> as you grow
> older be a counsel
> for others."

. . . 50 years later.

They're all around you—people who have shared directly or indirectly in your development as an individual. Parents, teachers, employers, associates—all have invested in you. They want you to succeed. And in many ways, they know you better than you know yourself. You benefit, therefore, by drawing on their experience and wisdom.

There's an old saying, "If we don't learn from history, we're bound to repeat it." History exists within the context of your family, and your parents and grandparents have lived it. History exists within the context of your business, and your employer or older associates probably have lived

Show Respect for Elders and Seek Counsel from
Those Who Are Older and Wiser

that as well. Learn from their successes and their failures. Seek the counsel of your elders, and as you grow older be a counsel for others.

During my Air Force days we lived in various places across the country and were almost always able to find an older couple to serve as mentors. Amy and I as well as our young children benefited from their years of wisdom by spending time with them. As Amy and I grew older, it seemed natural for us to fulfill this same role for others. Over the years we have looked for opportunities to teach young married couples in the churches we have attended.

Show Respect for Elders and Seek Counsel from
Those Who Are Older and Wiser

The Bible clearly states that older women are to teach younger women, and older men are to teach younger men. I always look forward to the next opportunity to help someone with less life experience than myself, and I still seek the chance to learn from those with more.

Show Respect for Elders and Seek Counsel from Those Who Are Older and Wiser

Denis and Esther in 1968 and in 1998 at their son's wedding reception. They have been married for 36 years.

The 6th Commandment...

YOU SHALL NOT MURDER.

— **6** —

Show Respect for One Another and Love One Another

When you marry, you promise to love each other "for better or worse, for richer or poorer, in sickness and in health until death do you part." Times will come in your marriage when this love is tested—times when the emotion and feelings are not high. But this type of love is not based on feelings. It is a decision. It is a choice you make, and it is for life.

I've said many times that Amy and I didn't "love" each other enough when we married to make it through fifty-five years. I usually get quizzical looks in response.

"What do you mean, you didn't love each other enough?" people ask. "You've been married half a century.

I've never seen a couple more in love!"

I explain that the love we share now did not exist in such large measure in our beginning. We thought we loved each other, certainly. But looking back and considering the kind of love and the amount of love we shared, if we had had to depend on that to bind us together through decades good and bad, lean and fat, our marriage would have dissolved long ago.

What we did have the day we married, though, was a commitment to each other and to our marriage. We accepted our responsibility to one another, and as we fulfilled that

Alan and Shirley—Halloween 1962. Just engaged . . .

> "[Marriage] is a choice you make, and it is for life."

. . . married 36 years.

responsibility our love grew. Underlying our love is a deep sense of respect for the worth and dignity of each other. We encourage each other, and neither of us criticizes the other in private or in public.

God gave the commandment, "You shall not murder." Christ clarified the commandment when He said, "Everyone who is angry with his brother will be liable to judgment."

How appropriate His words are to marriage. You can murder each other so easily with your angry, critical words. You pierce the spirit of your spouse again and again, day after day, then you refuse the first aid of heartfelt apology and encouragement. And from each wound you inflict, love bleeds, until one day you look at each other and the love has run dry. Then somebody says, "I'm leaving you."

When we destroy each other's self-worth and self-respect, we are forced into a position of self-contempt—a position that eventually will break up our marriage. Do not allow this to happen. Keep an environment of respect and love in your home every day and your marriage will flourish.

This can be difficult in a marriage where one or both personalities lacks a people-focus. Amy and I, for example, are both highly task-oriented, but in different ways. Amy

Richard and Laura in 1973 . . .

> "Keep an environment of respect and love in your home every day and your marriage will flourish."

. . . and in 1998. Married 24 years.

says, "Let's do it the right way." I say, "Let's do it my way." As you might imagine, we can quickly fall into conflict when we work together on a project.

That is when we rely on our values and the principle stated here, "Show respect for each other and love one another." That is where God's character comes in, His character of love.

Love, to us, is showing responsibility to each other—discussing issues of disagreement without anger or resentment. We've found that when we act this way, our love grows.

I must admit that occasionally we tend to attack each

other. If I lose control I will criticize, and Amy does not handle criticism well. Before we know it, we've started World War III in our home unless one or both of us turns to our values, which are a function of God's principles and God's character.

Children, particularly teenagers, compound this difficulty as they try to play father against mother and vice versa. Consequently, it's important to let the children know that your spouse is a higher priority than they are. The mother and father both must support this position.

Show Respect for One Another and Love One Another

The 7th Commandment...

YOU SHALL NOT COMMIT ADULTERY.

— 7 —

Maintain the Proper Physical Relationship

The foundational institution in every culture and society is the family unit, and marital fidelity is fundamental to the success of the family unit. The powerful sexual relationship is also the weak point the enemy will exploit to destroy your marriage. So how do you protect yourself?

Amy and I have always been committed to each other and each other alone. Because sin is a part of human nature, there are times when I think or behave in ways that I should not. A man is wired up to lust. But if I experience lust for a woman other than Amy, I tell God about it. I say, "Please help me deal with this right now," because if I don't, it won't go away. And every time I've said that to God, He's given me a distraction to put those other thoughts out of my mind.

My actions can also keep me out of situations that might lead to lust and its ensuing complications. Of course, I grew up in the John Wayne generation, where men didn't eat quiche or drink white wine, and they kissed the horse instead of the girl. Perhaps that was helpful, because I never allow another woman to hug me. I've been privileged to speak to many groups around the world, and quite often when I finish a lady will come up and say, "Oh, you were just wonderful. I want to give you a big hug." And I say, "No ma'am, only my wife does that." I realize that hugging most often carries no sexual meaning, but why take chances?

You may think lust is harmless. "Just looking," you say. But that "look" is a crack in your armor, and through the crack seeps opportunity. Maybe not now, maybe not next year, but you let enough opportunity seep through the crack and eventually lust will form and you'll weaken and break.

How can we risk everything so easily? Why even start down that road by "just looking?" The Bible says, "Flee!"

A publicly committed marriage of a man to a woman is a desirable institution. Children are a benefit of that union and an invaluable asset to the relationship. The family unit is the greenhouse for growing commitment, convictions, communications, companionship, and a personal value system.

So many people destroy so much for so little.

The 8th Commandment...

YOU SHALL NOT STEAL.

— 8 —
Face the Financial
Issues Together

A marriage is like a corporate merger: everything you own and everything your spouse owns becomes part of the new corporation.

A couple I counseled recently illustrates the importance of this principle. Each of them owned a condominium when they married, and they both agreed that they would sell one and live in the other.

Well, by the time they came to me, the wife was indignant. "He sold my condo and lost the money in a bad investment," she explained.

In her mind, as soon as things went bad financially

"we" became "he," and "our" became "my."

Further questioning of the couple revealed that the husband had, indeed, made a bad choice—one with which the wife disagreed. So, they had several issues to work through.

First, there is no "mine" and "yours" in a marriage. It is all "ours."

Second, although the husband might have the authority—even biblical authority—to make financial decisions for the family, he must consider his wife's opinion and his decision's impact on her. They should discuss major investments and, if they cannot agree, attempt to reach a

Bob and Bridgett in 1979...

"Create a good financial plan, one that you can agree on, then work together to implement it. Make it your goal to avoid the burden of debt and wisely manage the resources you've been given."

. . . 18 years later.

compromise each can be comfortable with.

This point is particularly important in this day when so many people are investing in the stock market for their retirement. Most money managers will determine their clients' aversion to risk and suggest investment alternatives accordingly. Likewise, a husband should consider his wife's risk aversion when investing. In this case, the husband did not, and I believe the wife was not only mad, but fearful of future mistakes.

Third, once the decision is made, a wife or husband should never say, "I told you so." If things go badly, as I mentioned earlier in the book, the words most wives need to hear most are, "I love you." Men, on the other hand, need to hear, "I believe in you."

Wives, don't let financial mistakes shake your confidence in your husbands.

Husbands, discuss with your wives important financial and career issues. Just remember, wives usually prefer security while husbands are attracted to risk.

In this couple's case, the woman had been working for several years and had built considerable equity in her condominium before the marriage. She understood finances and investing, just as many wives do. She and her husband should work as a team in managing their finances.

Now, what are their choices? You can do five things with money: pay taxes, pay debts, live off of it, accumulate it, or give it away.

Create a good financial plan, one that you can agree on, then work together to implement it. Make it your goal to avoid the burden of debt and wisely manage the resources you've been given.

Amy and I were fortunate on this point. We both grew up during the Depression years, so we learned the value of money. Plus, my father always taught me to stay out of debt. He had me so convinced, I thought debt was against the law.

Amy managed our resources when the Air Force called me away. She also worked as a bookkeeper for her father, and consequently understood what the Proverb said about the king who loses his riches quickly if he doesn't have someone to keep count of his sheep and goats. Of course, military pay didn't allow the accumulation of many "sheep and goats," but we did establish a standard of living that would give us the freedom to do the things that we believed God wanted us to do.

It was Amy who taught me the value of tithing. When we were teenagers, she worked part-time at Kresse's department store making $1.50 a week. When I went to church with her on Sunday, she put fifty cents in the plate—one-third of everything she'd earned that week. Over time I came to understand that God doesn't own just the 10 percent or the 33 percent. God owns it all.

He has blessed us with good health and with nine grand-children, and we prefer those blessings to material things.

The 9th Commandment...

YOU SHALL NOT GIVE FALSE
TESTIMONY AGAINST YOUR NEIGHBOR.

—9—
Demonstrate Honesty and Integrity

*P*ersonal honesty and integrity are the fundamental building blocks for any relationship, especially your marriage relationship. Only in an atmosphere of commitment and trust can your marriage prosper in all aspects: physically, emotionally, and spiritually.

When I was in Vietnam, I didn't worry about things at home because I knew I had a wife who was honest and had integrity. I knew that she was supporting me and taking care of the home front. Likewise, she knew that I was a person of integrity—that she could trust me when I was away for months at a time.

Demonstrate Honesty and Integrity

Unfortunately, many of my colleagues did not have that trust in their marriages. They wondered what their wives were doing back home and who they were doing it with. At the same time, some of them lived a life in Vietnam that betrayed many, if not all, of their marriage vows. I often wondered if their wives, thousands of miles away, suspected. How miserable they both must have been.

Telling the truth has always been a positive factor in our marriage. In the short haul it may sometimes factor in better to tell a little lie to keep peace in the marriage. But over time it doesn't work. The problem becomes one of

*Michael and Ruth in 1943, the
year they were married . . .*

"When the truth is
bad news, . . . face
it together and
draw strength
from one another."

. . . the couple 2 years before Michael's death. They were married 54 years.

remembering everything you've said. When you tell the truth, you never have to remember what you say. You just tell the truth.

I believe husbands lie more often than wives do, usually in an attempt to protect their wives from something stressful or hurtful. I don't believe in that kind of "protection." Amy doesn't need my protection from the truth. She's strong, and she can stand up to it just as I can. When the truth is bad news, we face it together and draw strength from one another.

Be truthful in the little things as well. Husbands, if you

tell your wife you'll be home for dinner at 7 p.m., be there. Let your ayes be ayes and your nays be nays.

In addition to eroding trust in the marriage, lies also teach children, who catch on quickly, that it's okay to lie. You tell a white lie, they see it, then they start doing it. Except they don't know the difference between a white lie and a black lie.

And you know what? There is no difference. A lie is a lie is a lie.

Keep them out of your marriage, out of your home.

Pete and Linda—just married—May 18, 1968 . . .

> "Personal honesty and integrity are the fundamental building blocks for any relationship, especially your marriage relationship."

... married 30 years.

The 10th Commandment...

YOU SHALL NOT COVET YOUR NEIGHBOR'S HOUSE. YOU SHALL NOT COVET YOUR NEIGHBOR'S MANSERVANT OR MAIDSERVANT, HIS OX OR DONKEY, OR ANYTHING THAT BELONGS TO YOUR NEIGHBOR.

— 10 —
Be Content with Yourself and Your Marriage

Let's face it, we live in a "more is better" society. Get more! Get more! Get more! More of everything. More money. More house. More cars. A more youthful wife.

We see pictures in magazines, on television, in movies, on billboards, of all the things everybody should have. With the pictures comes the pitch: if you don't have all this great stuff, you're a failure.

And who wants to be a failure?

Well, if American society at the end of the twentieth century is the judge, paint Amy and me failures. Proud failures.

As I mentioned in the eighth principle, the Air Force

did not offer tremendous monetary rewards for success. When I retired, Amy and I decided to continue that standard of living. We bought a comfortable home in a beautiful neighborhood with a good mix of young couples and retirees. That decision gave us the freedom to be available for others, particularly our family, and for God. I don't have to charge huge sums to speak, and I can run the Executive Leadership Foundation without worrying about whether it generates income for my family.

So instead of judging us by late twentieth-century American standards, Amy and I would rather you ask our

Walter and Pearl in their Sunday best in 1959 . . .

" . . . Accept each other just as you are and . . . behave responsibly to one another."

. . . married 60 years.

two children or our nine grandchildren or our friends and neighbors and co-workers if we have succeeded.

Contentment within a marriage can be even harder to maintain than contentment within one's self. After two or three years you begin to notice a slight flaw in your spouse, but you say, "No problem, I'll straighten it out."

More years go by and you discover you haven't made a dent in straightening out your spouse. The wife or husband hasn't changed. And you ask yourself, "What am I going to do?"

Some people will say, "I can't live with this flaw. I have

to get out." And suddenly it's over. Divorce. The children suffer most in this scenario.

There's a second alternative. You could put up with the other person and his or her so-called faults, and live together until the children leave home and you're left with two strangers in the house. Then you look at each other across the breakfast table one morning and say, "Let's split." In this case you have broken-hearted grandchildren and disillusioned children.

The third option is to accept each other just as you are and to behave responsibly to one another. Amy and I try every day to teach each other these ten principles by our behavior. Most of all, we enjoy our companionship. After fifty-five years our love, our friendship, and our respect for one another still grows.

We pray the same for you.

SUMMARY

Teaching the Third Generation

When applied, the principles we've outlined demonstrate the biblical model for marriage, the institution that God created before the church or state. And the challenge of Ephesians 5 and Psalm 78 will be met. Then your grandchildren will look and see how their grandparents are behaving. And you will have taught the third generation as it is explained in Psalm 78. Fathers (now, I also assume that is mothers) are to teach their children God's principles, and they will in turn teach their children God's principles.

Three generations. That is the source of stability for society. All the other efforts have failed in vain. Public education can't do it. The church can't do it. The government can't do it. Everyone is trying, but institutions do not change society—individuals do. And the individuals are a husband and a wife who understand the principles and who apply them in their daily lives. Then as they are sitting in the rocking chair together, with fifty-something years of marriage behind them, their love will be greater than ever. And their grandchildren will say that Grandmommy and Granddaddy really love each other. That is the key to marriage.

Make personal the application of these ten wonderful principles given to us by the God of Abraham, Isaac, and Jacob, and brought down off the mountain top by that great prophet and leader Moses. The principles in the absolute form are God's Ten Commandments.

CONCLUSION

Love Satisfies God's Commandments.
It Is the Only Law You Need.
Romans 13:10 (paraphrased)

Amy and I are totally convinced that these principles are as unchanging as the law of gravity. We also believe that fifty-five years of application of these principles prove that they work. They are the foundation for marriage, business, and life. Please learn them and teach them to your children and your children's children. God bless you!

. . . so that you, your children and their
children after them may fear the Lord
your God as long as you live by keeping all
His decrees and commands that I give you,
and so that you may enjoy long life.

—Deuteronomy 6:2

THE AUTHORS

1942–During their dating days . . .

. . . Married 55 years.

ABOUT THE AUTHORS

Mac McNair is a former career Air Force officer, professor at North Carolina State University, and director of aerospace programs at the Pentagon. A former member of the Board of Directors of the American Association of Bible Colleges and the founding president of Executive Ministries, a division of Campus Crusade for Christ, he currently is president of McNair Associates, a management consulting firm, and chairman of the Executive Leadership Foundation.

Amy McNair, a homemaker, teaches classes with Mac on the principles for a successful marriage.

They live near Atlanta, Georgia.